Triumphant Prayer Guide

Volume 1

The Sound of God's Army

Marilyn Robert

ACKNOWLEDGMENTS

I want to express my deepest thanks to my Battle Buddy Prophetess Pamela Hill who has diligently stood with me in many battles. I would also like to thank all of my intercessors who have fought the good fight with me.

I want to give special acknowledgment to Sharon Newson for helping me get this manuscript ready for publication:

Preface

Triumphant Prayer Guide is a tool that is designed to equip people to be *triumphant, steadfast* and *unmovable* during spiritual battles. This tool is loaded with biblical ammunition and militant prayer strategies that will posture you to stand as a triumphant warrior for Christ.

About the Author

I will start with a little history of my journey to becoming a triumphant warrior for Christ. Growing up as a young child I lived a painful life. At the age of four, I was brutally molested with a large bottle that destroyed my female body parts and organs. Life didn't stop nor did the pain and anger. As I grew up and became older I took on the identity of the person that molested me. In 1995, I accepted Jesus Christ as my Lord and Savior, but I was still trapped in the prison of the pain and anger from my child-age years.

In 1996 I was baptized by the Spirit of God with evidence of speaking in tongues and power. The Lord clothed me with a prayer mantle for the nations on October 27, 1997. The Spirit of God came to me in a vision on October 27, 1997. This night He also birthed in me *Pray for The Nations of People Ministry*. In the vision I saw an eagle with an eyeball in its mouth. There was a sound coming from the mouth of the eagle. It was the voice of the Spirit of God which spoke to me saying "Marilyn arise and pray for all 194 countries and 57 territorial islands overseas. Pray repentance, salvation, deliverance, and love [to] rule, and reign upon the heart of man."

I am commissioned by God to equip intercessors and people of prayer to stand on the walls of all nations to conquer territories for the advancement of God's Kingdom. We are a people of prayer for all nations and islands.

I serve as the Director of Intercessory Prayer at Center for Manifestation. I am the Founder of both the Jesus Military Forces Academy and of 7 Mountains Radio Broadcast.

CONTENTS

1

Triumphant Prayer Keys

There is no doubt that God was aforetime ready to respond to the pleading of His people and perform great triumphs through them. *Triumphant Prayer Keys* is design to access and unlock God's triumphant wisdom and utilize its keys.

Triumphant Prayer Keys:

God is the one who fights your battles:

Deuteronomy 20:4 *For the LORD your God is he who goes with you to fight for you against your enemies, to give you the victory.*

During spiritual battles, the born-again Christian must know that God is aware of the spiritual battles we are to face. When we understand and know that God is aware of our spiritual battles, we are then positioned in trust and faith. Knowing that God is with us in the battle and the battle is not our but it is the Lords, allows us to become or remain rooted and grounded while in a spiritual battle.

What does it look like to be rooted and grounded while in spiritual battle? This person is a Christian that is anchored in the identity of Christ. He or she has faith in the Word of God and the finished work of Jesus Christ.

God is the Power of your Prayers:

What does this mean? If you are praying and there is no presence of God, there is no power. Without God, there is no power!

The power of prayer is communicating with an unseen God through your unseen spirit Man. I call this kind of power Spirit to Spirit power that manifests result in the natural earthly realm as it is in Heaven.

Isaiah 1:24 *Therefore the Lord GOD of hosts, The Mighty One of Israel, declares, "Ah, I will be relieved of my adversaries and avenge myself on my foes.*

When born-again Christians call on the Lord GOD of hosts, He is so gracious that He is always there and available. This is achieved through our faith in the Lord Jesus Christ.

Jesus Christ, the King of glory, is the commander of the army of heaven and will eventually defeat all His enemies in this world.

There are Angels assigned to you to help:

There are other Spiritual beings assigned to you. Some are sent from heavenly realms to assist you while others are ungodly and meant for your demise.

Matthew 18:18, Jesus gave the church the keys of the kingdom of heaven. He said,

" Whatever you bind on earth will be bound in heaven, and whatever you loose on earth will be loosed in heaven".

Jesus said that we have the power to bind and loose.

When born-again Christians are seated in Christ we have the authority to loose Angels. The purpose and assignment of these Angels of God are to assist the born-again Christian in spiritual battles.

Spiritual battles are fought in spiritual realms and kingdoms. The Battle Headquarter for the born-again Christian is in the third Heaven. Here is where we are seated as a commander in Christ.

When born-again Christians are seated in the commanders' seat of Christ, we have spiritual insight to see Satan's war plans. We also have spiritual vision to see God's plans for the war to defeat Satan.

During spiritual battles, born-again Christians have spiritual ability to command God's angels and to dispatch and do battle against Satan's demonic agents.

Psalm 103:20 it says, *"Bless the Lord, ye his angels that excel in strength, that do his commandments, hearkening unto the VOICE of his word.*

A born-again person that is seated in Christ is a Christian that speaks on behalf of Jesus Christ. The angels of God obey the voice of God spoken through the born-again Christian.

The passage of scripture that paints this picture of the unseen reality for us is found in 2 Kings 6:17.

"And Elisha prayed, "Open his eyes, LORD, so that he may see." Then the LORD opened the servant's eyes, and he looked and saw the hills full of horses and chariots of fire all around Elisha".

The angels of God and ungodly angels are seen through the eyes of the Christians spirit man. The born-again Christians spirit man has the ability to see and hear in spiritual realms. This is a supernatural sight, and cannot be done in the natural.

Know that you are anointed and have been given authority:

Luke 10:19 *Behold, I have given you authority to tread on serpents and scorpions, and [authority] over all the power of the enemy, and nothing will injure you.*

God is revealing through Luke 10:19 the spiritual ammunition (authority) that He has given born-again Christians over all of Satan's power. The revelation of this verse is that Satan knows that God has given born-again Christians His authority and power to rule and reign.

God's anointing is for everyone that is yoked by sin and Satan's strongholds. It is through the anointing that we are set free from yokes.

Isaiah 10:27 *It shall come to pass in that day, that his burden shall be taken away from off your shoulder, and his yoke from off your neck, and the yoke shall be destroyed because of the anointing.*

Be bold and courageous:

As a military leader, Joshua was considered to be one of the greatest generals in human history. However, God still encouraged Joshua to be strong and courageous. In the midst of spiritual battles, we need to be encouraged by God.

Preparation before spiritual battles.

Encouraging words are fuel for your ammunition which is boldness.

Joshua 1:9 *Have I not commanded you? Be strong and courageous. Do not be afraid; do not be discouraged, for the LORD your God will be with you wherever you go.*

Jude 1:20 *you, dear friends, by building yourselves up in your most holy faith and praying in the Holy Spirit.*

God's strength is available to you:

Psalm 29:11 *The LORD will give strength to His people; The LORD will bless His people with peace.*

God has made His strength available to us in our weakness and in battles.

How does one embrace the strength of God? This is done by creating a spiritual appetite in the Word of God, in worship, and in prayer the born-again Christian can embrace Gods strength.

Isaiah 40:29-31 *He gives strength to the weary, and to him who lacks might He increases power. Though youths grow weary and tired, and vigorous young men stumble badly, yet those who wait for the LORD Will gain new strength; They will mount up with wings like eagles, they will run and not get tired, they will walk and not become weary.*

Seated in Heavenly Places in Christ:

Ephesians 2:6 says,

" And hath raised us up together, and made us sit together in heavenly places in Christ Jesus".

We are seated with Christ in heavenly places. Joint seating with Christ is far above all principalities and powers of darkness. Evil spirits can't influence believers who are seated with Christ in heavenly places.

This, the commander's seat of heavenly places, is a place where we legislate the kingdom of God from Heaven to the earth.

Our seating and reigning with Christ is a position of *authority, honor, and triumph.*

Ephesians 3:10 tells of God's triumphant promise to the church. God's intent was that now, through the church, the manifold wisdom of God should be made known to the rulers and authorities in the heavenly realms. These rulers and authorities are Satan's demonic agents. Through Christ Jesus, we have authority over Satan's kingdom and his demonic agents.

The key words in this verse are *the manifold Wisdom of God.* This wisdom is seen in Jesus Christ when He conquered and triumphed over death. The manifold wisdom of God is our triumphant weapon over Satan, demonic spirits, and his kingdom.

Pray in the Spirit:

The Spirit of God lives in the Spirit of the born-again Christian. His [Christian] spirit has a language and the Bible describes this language as speaking in tongues or a heavenly language.

When born-again Christians pray in the spirit, his spirit is communing with God's Spirit. This is the essence of spirit communication.

Praying in the Spirit is a powerful and triumphant prayer key. This kind of prayer helps us in our weakness.

Romans 8:26, 27 *Likewise the Spirit helps us in our weakness. For we do not know what to pray for as we ought, but the Spirit himself intercedes for us with groaning too deep for words. And he who searches hearts knows what is the mind of the Spirit because the Spirit intercedes for the saints according to the will of God.*

There is Power in the Name of Jesus:

Praying in Jesus' name is what I want to bring to the forefront. Jesus has invited, urged, and commanded us to pray in his name and the scriptures reveal to us that we will triumph in Jesus' name. The name of Jesus is our badge of authority in the earth. His name is a triumphant key that is available to born-again Christians.

The Scriptures declare in Jesus' name:

- devils were powerless. (Luke 10:17).
- the demons were cast out (Mark 16:17-18).
- healing occurred (Acts 3:6, 3:16, 4:10).
- salvation comes (Acts 4:12, Rom. 10:13).
- we are to baptized (Matt. 28:19).
- we are justified (1 Cor. 6:11).
- everything we do and say is done (Col. 3:17).

Apply the Blood of Jesus:

The Blood of Jesus is our triumphant key to overcome Satan and his demonic agendas. We witness the power of the Blood of Jesus throughout many scriptures in the Bible.

The shed Blood of Jesus speaks a language of triumph. Let's view Jesus' triumphant journey.

1. Luke 22: 1-6 Jesus Triumphant over Judas betrayal.
2. Luke 22: 7-38 Jesus Triumphant at the last supper.
3. Luke 22:39-46 Jesus Triumphant when He prayed at Mount Olive.
4. Luke 22:47-53 Jesus Triumphant when He was arrested.
5. Luke 22:54-62 Jesus Triumphant when Peter disowns him.
6. Luke 22:63- 65 Jesus Triumphant when the guards mocked Him.
7. Luke 22:66-71 Jesus Triumphant before Pilate and Herod
8. Luke 23:26-43 Jesus Triumphant during the crucifixion.

9. Luke 23:44-49 Jesus Triumphant over death.
10. Luke 24:1-12 Jesus Triumphant as He rises from the dead.
11. Death could not hold Him in the grave.
12. Luke 24:50-53 Jesus Triumphant as he ascends into heaven.

2

Triumphant in your Soul

The Body of Christ has to recover their soul and remain triumphant in their soul.

Key Words:

Triumph: A conclusive success following an effort, conflict, or confrontation of obstacles; victory; a state of joy or exultation at success.

Triumphant: having won a battle or contest; victorious.

Defeat: To overcome in battle or contest. To reduce, to nothing, the strength of.

Stronghold: A stronghold is anything that exalts itself in our minds, pretending to be bigger or more powerful than God.

A stronghold as stated in 2 Corinthians 10:5, is built by the imagination and every high thing that exalts itself against the knowledge of God.

As God is a tri-part Father, Son, and Holy Spirit, so man is three parts, Body, Soul and Spirit.

Man Soul:

Genesis 2:7 *And the Lord God formed man of the dust of the ground, and breathed into his nostrils the breath of life; and man became a living soul.*

The body part of a man is physical material [flesh] and is made to function on the earth.

The soul part of man is the intangible, spiritual part of a human being. The soul is comprised of the three parts mind, emotion, and will.

The mind is a part of the human soul. This is the part that reasons, thinks, feels, perceives, judges, and houses intelligence.

Another part of the human soul is the emotion. This part is an effective state of consciousness in which joy, sorrow, fear, hate, or like emotions are experienced.

The final part of the human soul is ones will. This part is the human choice or desires. I call this part the appetite factor because the human will crave what it desires.

Works of the Flesh:

The works of the flesh are keys that give access to demonic spirits that are sent to fragment the soul. These sins beat against the soul and cause the soul to become damaged and broken.

Galatians 5:19-21

The acts of the flesh are obvious: sexual immorality, impurity and debauchery; idolatry and witchcraft; hatred, discord, jealousy, fits of rage, selfish ambition, dissensions, factions and envy; drunkenness, orgies, and the like. I warn you, as I did before, that those who live like this will not inherit the kingdom of God.

Fragmented Souls Identified:

When a soul is fragmented it is a broken damaged soul. The mind, emotion and will do not have the ability to function normally. They function under the control of what has caused the fragmented soul.

What causes a Fragment Soul?

1. Sin, and any form of abuse. (Sexual, emotional, physical or mental).
2. Being forced to act against your morals.
3. Entering a relationship without strong boundaries of self, resulting in an unhealthy relationship and losing your personal power.
4. Deep depression and stress.
5. Physical and mental illness or infirmities.
6. An event of prolonged grief, pain, anger and fear that made you feel helpless or impotent.
7. Deeply seated addictions such as substance dependency.
8. An experience of intense rejection or abandonment.

9. A sudden and shocking accident.
10. A near death or out of body experience
11. Demonic practice, witchcraft, occult, and sorcery.
12. Witnessing the unexpected death of someone.
13. Identity crisis is a result of a fragmented soul.
14. Fragmented souls can also occur when an embryo is developing in the womb because of the amount of damage to the mothers' soul.

Soul Recovery:

Restoration: the action of returning something to a former owner, place, or condition. Repair, repairing, fixing, rebuilding, mending, reconstruction.

During the soul recovery process, there are two stages of restoration. The first stage is acknowledging that you need restoration and the second stage is being restored for God's use or work. What does acknowledgment look like? Forgiving yourself and putting God in charge of your soul.

I call the first stage of soul Restoration "The Potter's House encounter". When a born-again Christian allows God to be in charge of their soul, and forgives himself or herself, what they are saying to God is "you are the potter and my soul is the clay mold and make me again God".

As you read Jeremiah 18:1-4 see yourself as clay and God the Potter.

This is the word that came to Jeremiah from the LORD: Go down to the potter's house, and there I will give you my message." So I went down to the potter's house, and I saw him working at the wheel. But the pot he was shaping from the clay was marred in his hands; so the potter formed it into another pot, shaping it as seemed best to him. Deliverance: The act of being rescued or set free. Psalm 6:4 Return, O Lord, deliver my soul: oh save me for Thy mercies' sake.

During the deliverance [restoration] process, the born-again Christian must confess sin, faults, and all issues that have caused damage to the soul. They must repent. When the person turns to God with genuine repentance they will be set free.

The born-again Christian must renounce or disown sin. When he or she renounces sin the process of uprooting sin begins.

The process of deliverance looks similar to when a farmer prepares to plant his crops. The farmer must first prepare the ground by using plows or cultivators. I prefer the cultivator because a cultivator turns the ground over and removes the roots, weeds and other substances that are attached to the things that you are seeking to be delivered from. The cultivator separates the ground to prepare the ground for planting.

Healing: My definition of healing looks like this. Removing old contaminated soil and replacing it with fresh, new soil that is healthy for planting. The old contaminated soil is sin or whatever has caused damage to the soul. The new soil is the word of God that is planted in the soul to be rooted. If there is no repair to the soul (healing), the remnants of the old contaminated soil (sin) will still produce its kind.

Psalm 147:3 *He heals the brokenhearted and binds up their wounds.*

In order to be a triumphant warrior for Christ, you must gain the battleground of your mind, emotion, and will.

The mind is the battleground of the soul. This is the place where Satan attacks and fragments the soul.

Satan often attacks us by planting in our minds the idea that we can't trust God. Every sin can be traced back to that one deceptive thought. Since what you think ultimately becomes what you do, it's vital to pray regularly for the Holy Spirit to renew your mind.

Romans 12:2 *do not conform to the pattern of this world, but be transformed by the renewing of your mind. Then you will be able to test and approve what God's will is-- his good, pleasing and perfect will.*

Soul recovery is a process. When the soul has been damaged the soul has to go through a process of restoration, deliverance, and healing. After this process is completed the soul is then in a place of rest and being rejuvenated or revived.

While the soul is being rejuvenated or revived the person must draw near to God and He will draw near to them. The more he draws near to God his soul comes to a resting place in God.

While the soul is in God's resting place He [God] begins to restore and mend the fragments of the soul. This is the process when the soul is in the hands of the potter.

During this process, God, Elohim, the Creator begins to mold every piece of the person's soul back together. God is the Potter and we are His clay.

While his hand is working on the soul of a man, He begins the deliverance process by removing the issues that caused the soul to be damaged.

What does the soul deliverance process look like? God arising as the breaker, the one who set the captives free.

Matthew 11:28-30 *Come to me, all who labor and are heavy laden, and I will give you rest. Take my yoke upon you, and learn from me, for I am gentle and lowly in heart, and you will find rest for your souls. For my yoke is easy, and my burden is light.*

Born-again Christians must pay attention to the condition of the soul. We must make daily choices that will expand our own soul, drawing us closer to God.

Daily Soul Recovery Commands:

1. Ask God to command His angels to tear down ancient battlegrounds that were passed down through your generational bloodline.

2. Ask God to command His angels to guard your soul against the wiles of the devil.

3. Cast down all demonic thoughts that exalts itself against the knowledge of God.

4. Pray to restore your fragmented soul.

Father, I ask You in the Name of Jesus Christ to send out angels to gather up the fragments of my soul and restore them to their rightful place in me (Psalm 7:2, 23:3). I ask You to loose into me and my family the spirits of the Lord: Wisdom, Counsel, Might, Knowledge, Fear of the Lord, Power, Love, Sound Mind, Grace, Peace and the Spirit of the Lord. Thank you, Father.

3

Triumphant over the Enemy

Why do born-again Christians use the word command when praying?

This word command is an authoritative order. God expects His sons to function like Him. We are ambassadors of Jesus Christ.

➤ **Daily Triumphant Commands:**

This day I command the God of War to stand before my enemies. Oh Lord release Your hand and dash my enemies into pieces and overthrow their powers.

Exodus 15:3, 7 *The Lord is a man of war; the Lord is His name. In verse 7 and in the greatness of Your excellence You have overthrown those who rise against You.*

Come on Warriors of Christ!

(*militant push*)

> **Daily Triumphant Commands:**

This day I command the zeal of God to stir up within me like unto Isaiah 42:13. *I shall stand as a (cont.) triumphant warrior in Christ Jesus and I will not be defeated.*

Isaiah 42:13 *The Lord shall go forth like a mighty man; He shall stir up His zeal like a man of war. He shall cry out, yes, shout aloud; He shall prevail against His enemies.*

Come on Warriors of Christ!

> **Daily Triumphant Commands:**

This day I command the Lord of hosts to go before me and make my crooked paths straight and place my feet on God's ordained pathway.

This day I command the right hand of God to break in pieces all demonic gates that stand in opposition against God's open doors for me.

I will go before you and make the crooked paths straight; I will break in pieces the

gates of bronze and cut the bars of iron."
(Isaiah 45:2)

Come on Warriors of Christ!

➤ **Daily Triumphant Commands:**

This day I command the cords of the wicked to be cut in pieces and I command the hand of righteousness to establish me in this day.

Many a time they have afflicted me from my youth; yet they have not prevailed against me ... The Lord (cont.) is righteous; He has cut in pieces the cords of the wicked."
(Psalm 129:2)

Come on Warriors of Christ!

➤ **Daily Triumphant Commands:**

This day I command the hand of God to lift me up above those who rise against me and establish me in the earth above my enemy.

It is God who avenges me, and subdues the peoples under me; He delivers me from my enemies. You also lift me up above those who rise against me; You have delivered me from the violent man." (Psalm 18:47) "

Come on Warriors of Christ!

> ➢ **Daily Triumphant Commands:**

This day in the courtroom of heaven I command Psalm 35:1-3. *I plead my cause, O Lord, with those who strive with me; fight against those who fight against me. Take hold of shield and buckler, and stand up for my help. Also, draw out the spear, and stop those who pursue me. Say to my soul, "I am your salvation.*

Come on Warriors of Christ!

Praise and Worship causes us to Triumph over our enemies

Psalm 27:6-14 *So I will triumph over my enemies around me. With shouts of joy, I will offer sacrifices in his Temple; I will sing, I will praise the Lord. Hear me, Lord, when I call to you! Be merciful and answer me! When you said, "Come worship me," I answered, "I will come, Lord." Don't hide yourself from me! Don't be angry with me; don't turn your servant away. You have been my help; don't leave me, don't abandon me, O God, my savior. My father and mother may abandon me, but the Lord will take care of me. Teach me, Lord, what you want me to do, and lead me along a safe path, because I have many enemies. Don't abandon me to my enemies, who attack me with lies and threats. I know that I will live to see the Lord's goodness in this present life. Trust in the Lord. Have faith, do not despair. Trust in the Lord.*

Praise and Worship is a weapon toward your enemy.

Praise is a weapon of war. When a born-again believer in Christ praises God this signifies victorious marching orders that cause the hand God to move and deal with your enemies.

When a born-again believer in Christ praises God with the clapping of hands or lifting hands before God this signifies hand warfare. The importance of these movements is that Satan understands this as a type of warfare praise.

Praise elevates your perspective, causing you to see from God's victorious vantage point.

Psalm 121:1-2 *I will lift up my eyes to the hills, from where does my help come? My help comes from the Lord, who made heaven and earth.*

Praise positions you in the courts of heaven were you become in harmony with the sounds of praise and thanksgiving.

Psalm 144:1 *Blessed be the LORD, my rock, who trains my hands for war, and my fingers for battle.*

Satan understands this kind of war language. When a born-again Christian engages in warfare praise your hands and fingers began to move and do battle against the enemy (Satan).

Praise is our victorious marching orders!

4

Triumphant Warriors for Christ

Triumphant warriors for Christ is the pattern of Jesus Christ's triumphant life. In this pattern are models that reveal to born-again Christians how to live and remain triumphant in Christ.

Triumphant Warriors Daily Militant Orders:

The key to growing as a triumphant warrior for Christ is wrapped in these three words, [the] Word, Worship, and Prayer.

- Triumphant warriors for Christ must be ready to die daily and take up their cross and follow Jesus Christ.

- Triumphant warriors for Christ must become the word of God by studying and applying the word of God.
- Triumphant warriors for Christ must live a persistent prayer life and engage in praying all kinds of prayers. Ephesians 6:18 *And pray in the Spirit on all occasions with all kinds of prayers and requests. With this in mind, be alert and always keep on praying for all the Lord's people.*
- Triumphant warriors for Christ must live to Worship God Elohim the Creator. When a triumphant warrior lives to worship God this person is taking a posture to become the very image of God.
- Triumphant warriors for Christ are disciple warriors. They look for opportunities to equip others to become triumphant warriors for Christ. They also stand in battle for others.
- Triumphant warriors for Christ are known in Satan's kingdom. They

have a reputation of ambassadors of Jesus of Christ.

- Triumphant warriors for Christ work with Christ from heavenly places. I call this place the commander's seat. This place is far above all principalities and kingdoms.
- Triumphant warriors for Christ are fully loaded with Jesus Christs' armor and ready at all times for the battle.

Ephesians 6:10- 17 (NIV) *Finally, be strong in the Lord and in his mighty power. Put on the full armor of God, so that you can take your stand against the devil's schemes. For our struggle is not against flesh and blood, but against the rulers, against the authorities, against the powers of this dark world and against the spiritual forces of evil in the heavenly realms.*

Therefore, put on the full armor of God, so that when the day of evil comes, you may be able to stand your ground, and after you have done everything, to stand. Stand firm then, with the belt of truth buckled around your waist, with the breastplate of righteousness in place, and with your feet fitted with the readiness that comes from the gospel of peace. In addition to all this, take up the shield of faith, with which you can extinguish all the flaming arrows of the evil one. Take the helmet of salvation and the sword of the Spirit, which is the word of God.

5

Triumphant Prayer

Triumphant Prayer

As triumphant warriors for Christ we are defense attorneys, appealing to the higher court on behalf of our defendants.

In the name of Jesus Christ, I stand in the courtroom of heaven appealing to the higher court on behalf of the body of Christ. I command the triumphant zeal of God to clothe the body of Christ with Jesus Christ triumphant garment. I legislate the DNA of the finished work of Jesus Christ be manifest in us now in Jesus Christ name. We declare and decree the triumphant power that flows through Jesus Christ now flows through us. We declare and decree the triumphant tenacity that flows through Jesus Christ now flow through us. We declare and decree Jesus Christ's triumphant authority flows through us now. We declare and decree we are steadfast, unmovable always abounding in every area of life in Jesus Christ name.

We Are Triumphant Warriors for Christ!

Coming soon

***Triumphant Prayer Guide*
Volume**

If you are interested in participating in

Triumphant Mentorship Program

- Triumphant Training
    - o Soul
    - o Over your enemy
    - o Prayer etc.
- One-on-one deliverance
- Becoming a warrior for Christ

Contact: <u>mrmarilyn.mr@gmail.com</u>

*all scripture references in this guide are taken from the King James version or the NIV version of the Holy Bible.

Made in the USA
Middletown, DE
10 February 2018